Marine Life For Young Readers

Schools of Fish

Contents

Text by Stanley L. Swartz
Photography by Robert Yin

DOMINIE PRESS
Pearson Learning Group

About Schools of Fish

A group of cows or horses is called a **herd**. A group of fish is called a school. Some schools have only a few fish.

◀ Small School of Snappers

Other schools have thousands of fish. Most schools are made up of the same kind of fish. There are 24,000 types of fish.

◀ Large School of Snappers

Vertebrates are animals with a backbone. Half of all the vertebrates in the world are fish. It is possible that some fish have still not been **discovered**.

◄ Small School of Fish with Jellyfish

Where Fish Live

Many fish are very colorful. Fish are found almost everywhere. They live in oceans, lakes, and rivers.

◄ School of Fish on Sand, Feeding

The Many Uses for Fish

Many fish are used for food. Large fish eat smaller fish, and people eat fish. Some fish are kept as pets in **aquariums**.

◀ School of Fish in Circular Formation

Fish and Their Fins

Most fish have fins. The **dorsal** fin is found on the back of some fish. This fin helps the fish keep its balance.

◀ School of Fish on a Reef

The **pectoral** fins are found on both sides of most fish. They help the fish swim. They also help with direction.

◀ School of Parrotfish

The **caudal** fin is the tail. It is used for steering. The caudal fins on these fish are colorful.

◄ School of Butterfly Fish

Breathing under Water

The **gills** on these fish are behind the head. Gills are used to take oxygen from the water. This allows fish to breathe under water.

◀ Fish on the Ocean Floor

Fish live in places where people need **assistance**. We have no gills, so we have to bring our own oxygen. This diver is swimming with a school of fish.

◄ Diver with a School of Fish

The Price of Pollution

Pollution is hurting our water. Pollution can kill fish. Laws have been passed to protect the **environment**.

◄ School of Fish on Hard Coral

Glossary

aquarium:	A tank or bowl used to keep fish
assistance:	Support or help
caudal:	Near the tail, or like the tail
discovered:	Found; seen
dorsal:	Located on the back
environment:	Where we live; our surroundings
gills:	Organs used to breathe under water
herds:	Groups of animals that have a common bond and live together
pectoral:	Located on the side
pollution:	Something that is harmful to plants and animals
vertebrates:	Animals with a backbone, or spine

Index